critical acclaim

"A charming book....Shows readers, with humor and zest, how to live in the now and change our futures. For most collections."
    —*Library Journal*

"*Zen and the Art of Happiness* is enthusiastically recommended and 'user friendly' reading for anyone seeking to enhance their spirituality, deal with life's stresses, and improve their physical, emotional, and spiritual well-being."
    —*Midwest Book Review*

"The big-bellied, somewhat eccentric laughing Buddha on the cover tells it all. The author does not believe that happiness depends on being the same size as models in the fashion magazines, finding the perfect mate, filling one's house with cutting-edge electronic gadgets, or studying meditation with the current 'it' guru....

"The book reflects a long-standing esoteric maxim: We create our own reality. What makes this work different from so many others is the personal energy, knowledge, and insight with which he communicates. He draws on Eastern and Western philosophy, modern science, and personal— sometimes catastrophic—experience to explain why believing circumstances will benefit us is what will, ultimately, cause this to be true.

"His life h̶a̶s̶ ̶ lenges he has

turned into opportunities. He does not lecture to us from a pedestal as an enlightened being. Instead, he speaks as one who has survived the muck and mire and retained his childlike wonder and enthusiasm. Prentiss beckons us to see the world through his eyes and share his joy. It is easy to believe it is possible."

—*New Age Retailer*

"Happiness can be a fickle thing. It can be a snug, magnetic garment, attracting more and more of the same, or it can be an ill-fitting gossamer veil flitting here and there. It all depends on one's psychology, karma, and attitude. This wonderful little book shows that we *can* overcome the obstacles to happiness. It's for those who want and need change—in expectations, habits, and outlook. Chris Prentiss teaches us how, with a joie de vivre that obviously comes from experience. Use his practical wisdom to get in the habit of being happy—every day. Put this book by your bedside and the Zen of happiness can be yours."

—*ReverseSpins.com*

z

And the Art of

e

Happiness

n

Zen

And the Art of

Happiness

Chris Prentiss

POWER PRESS
Los Angeles, California

Library of Congress Control Number: 2006903540

For information, address:

Power Press
6428 Meadows Court
Malibu, California 90265
Telephone: 310-392-9393
Email: info@PowerPressPublishing.com
Website: www.PowerPressPublishing.com

For foreign and translation rights, contact Nigel J. Yorwerth
Email: nigel@PublishingCoaches.com

ISBN: 978-0-943015-53-8

20   19   18   17   16   15   14

Cover design: Nita Ybarra
Interior design: Roger Gefvert

For Todd

happiness

The three Chinese characters pictured on the cover and throughout the interior of this book are often used together. Collectively, they denote "happiness." Individually, these characters mean:

GOOD LUCK

PROSPERITY

LONGEVITY

The jolly "Laughing Buddha" on the front cover is a depiction of the endearing and compassionate Buddha known in Japan as Hotei and in China as Pu-tai. Some say the jovial figure is based on an eccentric, wandering Zen beggar monk who lived over a thousand years ago and who is believed to be an incarnation of the bodhisattva Maitreya (the Future Buddha), called the "Loving One" or "Friendly One."

The Buddha's large pot belly symbolizes happiness, good luck, and abundance and he graces all with his joy and playful spontaneity.

contents

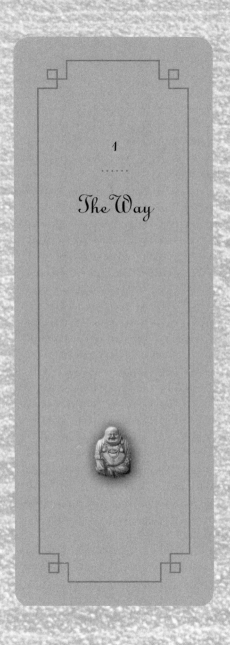

1

......

The Way

Perfection is

everywhere

if we only choose

to recognize it.

—OKAKURA KAKUZO

I | the way

THERE IS ONLY ONE WAY TO ACHIEVE LASTING happiness. That way is simply: Be happy.

After reading that, you might be having some or all of the following thoughts: "It's stupid, and I'm beginning to feel very unhappy about buying this book. I hope it gets better." "It's too simple." "The author has lost his mind and has taken to mumbling inanities." "It doesn't tell me enough about how I *get* to be happy." "Things just don't work like that." "It doesn't take into account the times when I'm decidedly *un*happy because of the inevitable mishaps and problems that arise in my everyday life, not to mention the tragedies." "You can't just *be* happy." "The author must be getting old."

All of that may be true. Being happy much more of the time than you have been is an incredibly complex and difficult task—not in the doing of it once you know how but in coming to know how and then in keeping aware of what you have discovered. Yet, I still say you *can* do it, and by the time you finish this little book, if you are willing to give what you have read a chance to be true, you *will* do it.

The path that has led to your current condition and situation was not a few days or months in the making, but a long and arduous path that has spanned many years. Actually, it has taken you as long as you've been alive to become the way you are. It has also taken you that long to achieve what you've achieved, to possess what you now possess, and to arrive at your current condition.

Your life today is the result of a series of decisions you made that have caused you to arrive where you are.

If who you are and what you have is what you want, if you're satisfied with the conditions of your life, congratulations—do more of what you've been doing and you'll get more of what you already have. But if who you are, what you want, what you have, and your current conditions are less than what you want or are different from what you want, you have to make some changes—basic changes, inner changes. Failure to make those changes will find you fruitlessly continuing to seek the things you desire as the years pass by.

In this book, you may see statements that are contrary to what you believe, contrary to what your experience has taught you, contrary to what others have told you, contrary to the spiritual traditions you grew up with, and even contrary to your own common sense. *That is to be expected.* If it were not that way, you would have already achieved the art of happiness.

Because some of what you will read may seem impossible or foolish, even ridiculous, it may at first offend your sensibilities, causing you to scoff at it, ridicule it, and reject it. Each time you come upon a statement that has that effect upon you, I suggest that before rejecting it, you ask yourself whether or not you would *want* that statement to be true—and then give yourself the chance to see it as true.

simple questions

> *The truth is always near at hand, within your reach.*
> —D. T. SUZUKI

With your permission, I would now like to take you beyond the limits of your customary thoughts and experiences. This new way of life begins with two simple questions.

First, answer truthfully the following question. *Would I want this to be true: "Every event that befalls me is absolutely the best possible event that could occur."*

The second, more difficult part, is to truthfully answer the question: *Will I give that a chance to be true?*

Imagine that God appeared before you this

instant and said: "I promise you that everything that happens to you from this moment forward will be of the greatest benefit to you and will bring you the utmost good fortune." Suppose God went on to say: "Even though what happens will sometimes appear unfortunate or hurtful, in the end your life will be wonderfully blessed and hugely benefited by *whatever* happens."

How would you feel about that wonderful news? Happy? Perhaps even joyful? Wouldn't it be the best piece of news you could hear? Wouldn't you heave a deep sigh of relief and feel as if a great burden had been lifted from your shoulders? Wouldn't you then respond to the next thing that happened—even if it was hurtful or took something from you or seemed bad or unlucky—as though it was going to be wonderfully beneficial for you, the best possible thing that could have happened?

If you did not enthusiastically answer *yes,* perhaps you have mistaken what I am talking about in the above paragraph. I am not talking about the phrase we commonly hear, "Try to make the best of it," which means "The situation or event really *is* bad and terribly unlucky, but do what you can to salvage some good out of it." Nor do I mean that within even the worst event possible, there can be found a tiny bit of good.

I am not thinking in terms of such limiting ideas. I am thinking in unlimited terms, where every event that befalls you is absolutely the best possible event that could occur—that there is no other event imaginable that could benefit you to any greater degree.

So, again, wouldn't that be the best piece of news you could hear? Wouldn't you heave a deep sigh of relief and feel as if a great burden had been lifted from your shoulders? And wouldn't you then respond to the next thing that happened—even if it was hurtful or took something from you or seemed bad or unlucky—as though it was the best possible thing that could have happened?

If you are willing to give this new concept a chance and to actually believe that everything that happens to you is the best thing that can possibly happen to you, you will start to act in accord with that belief and, as a result of natural law, bring about that end. It takes some getting used to and it takes presence of mind, which is the more difficult part, but the price is small considering the reward: a lifetime spent in the sunshine of happiness.

zen

Zen is simply...that state of centeredness which is here and now. —ALAN WATTS

Zen is too vast a subject to be dealt with in its entirety in this small book, but I will explore how the essence of Zen, its method, and its approach can be used effectively by us to achieve our goal of happiness.

Zen is a Japanese word that is derived from the Sanskrit word meaning "meditation" (*dhyana* in Sanskrit, *ch'an* in Chinese, and *zen* in Japanese). Zen is a journey of exploration and a way of living that, in and of itself, does not belong to any one religion or tradition. It is about experiencing life in the here and now and about removing the dualistic distinctions between "I" and "you," between "subject" and "object," between our spiritual and our ordinary, everyday activities. It is about seeing into, directly experiencing, and expressing one's true nature.

The Zen approach fosters a natural awareness and centeredness in our daily life. As D. T. Suzuki, the Japanese scholar and leading spokesman of Zen in mid-twentieth century America, said of Zen, "It merely enables us to wake up and become aware. It does not teach, it points."

Here is the heart of it:

The Zen of doing anything is doing it with a particular concentration of mind, a calmness and simplicity of mind, that brings the experience of enlightenment and, through that experience, happiness.

This book is about the Zen of happiness, which is another way of saying it's about the *art* of happiness, the *essence* of happiness, the *inner game* of happiness, the *inside track* to happiness.

Done correctly, happiness is an inevitable end.

In their efforts to experience enlightenment, yogis spend years and decades in meditation. Students of Zen concentrate for years on koans, or Zen riddles. The enlightened ones who attained their goal have attested that often the experience came in a flash and lasted only an instant, but it was so powerful that it changed them forever.

What did they experience that was so powerful? *Their oneness with the Universe.* That is what enlightenment is: knowing that everything in the Universe is created from and is part of the same energy, and knowing in what way we relate to it all. Once that awareness is obtained, all else falls into place, everything makes sense, and everything can be understood. As the Zen master Dogen taught, "To be enlightened is to be intimate with all things."

The goal of this book is to help you bring enlightenment into your life through understanding some of the most important laws that govern our world and the Universe, learning how those laws affect you, and then using that information to achieve happiness. The "concentration of mind" that characterizes Zen comes into play as you apply what you have discovered to every situation and event that affects your life.

Happiness that is achieved through an essential understanding of Universal laws and of our relationship to the Universe is true happiness. That kind of happiness endures and does not decrease with the changing conditions of time. It sees us through every difficulty, every loss, every hardship, and it brightens even our best days.

2

......

We Are
the Authors
of Every
Next
Moment

All that we are is the result

of what we have thought.

It is founded on our thoughts,

it is made up of our thoughts.

—THE DHAMMAPADA

2 | we are the authors of every next moment

WHAT HAS GONE BEFORE IN YOUR LIFE HAS MOST probably convinced you, first, that the statement "Everything that happens to me is the best possible thing that can happen to me" is not true and cannot be true and, second, that a book based in part on that premise is not going to do you much good. It may seem futile to even attempt to put that to the test.

But this is a new day. We have begun a new century and a new millennium, and you may discover in reading this book that it is your time to take on a new belief that will bless your life from this time onward.

We are the authors of every next moment.

We are powerful beings, creating our futures with our thoughts and actions. We are the mechanism by which life is controlled, and we control the events in our life by our personal philosophy, which determines how we respond to those events.

Each of us has a personal philosophy, but few of us have defined what it is. Although you may have never sat down and defined what your philosophy is, it is fully operative and working in your life at all times. It deals with what you believe about the world in which you live, about its people and events, about how events and circumstances affect you, and about how you affect them.

If you were asked about your philosophy of life in general, you might say, "Life is great, good things happen to me, I'm a lucky person, and I believe the world is a wonderful place with wonderful people in it." Or you might say just the opposite: "I'm unlucky, bad things happen to me, the world isn't a very nice place, people take advantage of me, and they're just out for what they can get." You might believe in Murphy's law—"If anything can go wrong, it will."

Many people say that bad accidents happen, that unfairness is not only possible but likely. They say that real happiness is hard to come by and usually short-lived, that we come into the world, live, and die and what we experience in between is mostly a struggle and a continual compromise between what we want and what we get.

Because that is what people have generally believed, their actions have been based on that belief and, as a result of natural law, they have brought about that end. Then they have said, "I told you so." They have not only "told you so," but they have also told everyone and everything else so, and thus it is so.

If you believe that something that happens to you is bad, you will react to the events in a way that will cause you more unpleasantness, and the unpleasantness you experience then appears to confirm that what happened was truly unfortunate. However, it was your reaction to the event that caused the continuation of the unpleasantness. *We are the ones who invest seemingly bad happenings with the power to seem bad at the time they occur and to continue to seem bad afterward.* As William Shakespeare wisely observed, "There is nothing either good or bad, but thinking makes it so."

Your personal philosophy determines how you respond to events that come into your life. It is completely responsible for your state of happiness and well-being. Although you may find this a little hard to believe, your personal philosophy also determines what happens to you. It has brought about all the past circumstances and most of the events of your life, even those you believe were outside your control, and it will continue to do so.

as you believe, so it is for you

The true man sees what the eye sees, and does not add to it something that is not there. He hears what the ears hear, and does not detect imaginary undertones or overtones. He...is not busy with hidden meanings. —CHUANG TZU

Acting on the basis of what you believe is what brings about the conditions of your life and the degrees of happiness you have experienced. In the breakthrough 2004 film *What the Bleep Do We Know!?*, physicist and author Fred Alan Wolf, Ph.D., observes: "There is no 'Out There' out there, independent of what goes on in our minds." Take the story of Max. Max owned a thriving sandwich shop. There were almost always people waiting in line to eat at his little shop. He gave away free pickles, free potato chips, sometimes a free soft drink, and his sandwiches were famous for being overstuffed.

One day his son, who lived in a distant city, came to visit. They had a good visit, but as the son was leaving, he told his father, "Since I've been here, I've been observing how you run the sandwich shop, and I have to tell you for your own good that you're making a big mistake giving away all those extras. The country's economy is in bad shape. People are out of work, and they have less money to spend. If you don't cut back on the free items and on your portion sizes, you'll be in a bad way before long too." His father was amazed, thanked his son, and told him he would consider his advice.

After his son left, Max followed his son's advice. He stopped giving away free items and he cut back on the generous portions of food in his sandwiches. Before long, after many of his disappointed customers had stopped coming, he wrote to his son: "You were right! The country's economy is in bad shape, and I'm experiencing the results of it right here in my sandwich shop!"

The poor economy that the man's son saw all around him was real. Despite the poor economy, though, the father had been running a successful sandwich shop. He didn't realize that times were hard, that many people were out of work, and that money was scarce. He was treating everyone with great generosity and he was reaping the rewards that such actions always bring: a positive, generous outpouring of good things. But after his son told him about the "bad shape" the country was in, he began to act as if it were so, bringing about the only possible result—a negative, fearful, ungenerous experience of life, an experience that he believed was "out there." Was it "out there"?

The answers are never "out there." All the answers are "in there," inside you, waiting to be discovered.

Here's a personal example of how the power of a belief can influence our behavior and the events of our lives. When I was young I received many speeding tickets, and that behavior carried over into my adult life. I live in California, and one day in 1968 I received a notice from the California Department of Motor Vehicles saying that if I received one more ticket, my license would be suspended for a year. The state suggested that I go to a local DMV office and meet with one of their psychologists. At the meeting, the psychologist commented on the many speeding tickets I had received.

"Everyone gets speeding tickets," I replied defensively.

"That's not true," he informed me. "The average person in California gets only one ticket every four years."

I was amazed. I thought that everyone was like me and got speeding tickets all the time. After that meeting, I stopped getting speeding tickets. I'd had a destructive mindset, and as I believed, so it was for me. As you believe, so it is for you.

You are like a railroad switch. Each time an event occurs, you channel the activity onto the positive or the negative track. Even though the event hurt you or took something away from you, you are still in charge of channeling it onto a positive or a negative track. You determine its future outcome.

Have you ever had anything happen to you that seemed really bad at the time but later turned out to be beneficial—experiences where days, weeks, or even years later, you said, "That was the best thing that could have happened to me!" Everyone I've ever posed that question to has been able to remember several events like that.

It's time to look at *all* events in the light of that information. Learn to see that perfect truth *now*, in *every* situation. Condition yourself to see it *at* the moment each event occurs, and happiness will become your constant companion. You will save countless hours, days, and weeks of useless lamenting over situations that will always turn out to be for your benefit.

3

······

The
New
Experience

Every day

is a good day.

—UMMON

3 | the new experience

HOW DO YOU CHANGE WHAT YOU BELIEVE WHEN your experience has convinced you otherwise?

By creating a new experience.

The best way for you to get that new experience is to change your response to what happens. By the natural law of cause and effect, that new response will create new results, which you will then experience as a new reality.

To reach the goal of happiness, act as though the following statement is true: *Everything that happens to me is the best possible thing that can happen to me.* It is as simple and unerring as: $1 + 1 = 2$.

> *Acting as though what happens to you is the best possible thing that can happen to you + the new results = happiness.*

When you are convinced of the truth that everything that happens is the best thing that can happen, life begins to be much more fun. It is like opening a direct channel to happiness.

Happiness is there, waiting for you. All you need to do is follow the formula that creates it. Unhappiness is also there, waiting for you. Your response determines which one you will experience.

Here is an example to help clarify how that principle works. Suppose you want to open a coffee shop and your budget is one hundred thousand dollars. Suppose you have that amount of money in the bank. You will go out looking for sites and start interviewing people for positions. You will get prices on equipment, look at furniture, contact sign makers, contact suppliers, arrange your schedule, and do all the things necessary to get the business started.

Imagine, instead, that you do not have the money in the bank. If you act on that fact, you'll do nothing except wonder how you can get the money to start the project. Knowing you do not have the money cripples your actions.

Now suppose that instead of allowing that to happen, you act as though you had the money in the bank. You start doing all the things you would do if you had the money. You start the project, and guess what? You create the conditions for the money to come. Maybe one of the people you interview wants to become a partner. Maybe one of the suppliers wants to put up the money. Maybe the landlord of the building you find likes you or your idea and wants to participate. Maybe the sign maker's brother-in-law is looking for an investment.

There is a phrase that encapsulates this approach to living that I have gleaned from the wisdom of the I Ching, an ancient Chinese text that dates back more than six thousand years:

Everything comes at the appointed time.

It's not necessary to have all the ingredients of a project in hand at the outset. They will come at the appointed time. It's only important that you move forward with the project until that appointed time arrives. With the energy you create by moving forward *as if* you had the money to start, you actually put into motion a stream of events that lead to your success. Your actions create an "energy vortex" that draws in the necessary ingredients for your venture.

Everything you need for your venture is, in actuality, already there, waiting for you—you only need to draw in what is needed. It is the same with happiness. Acting on the basis that everything happens only to benefit you creates an energy vortex that causes everything to benefit you. That result causes you to experience happiness, which then proves to you that this is how things really do work—and this leads you to believe that everything does indeed happen for your benefit. When you know that's true, that's when the deep sighs of relief come.

You will know that you have reached the

stage of acting as though what happens is the best possible thing that can happen when you realize, gradually or suddenly, that you have recently been happy most of the time, even though unpleasant events or circumstances have occurred.

the best possible thing

> *If you really know how to live, what better way to start the day than with a smile?...Smiling helps you approach the day with gentleness and understanding....Smile with your whole being.*
>
> —THICH NHAT HANH

The most difficult part in creating new results in our life is maintaining our awareness that whatever happens to us is for our greatest benefit. We tend to get caught up in whatever is going on and forget that we're supposed to be responding as though whatever is happening is the best possible thing that can happen to us. It takes work to remember, but it is the most rewarding work possible. One of the best ways to remember is to write on many pieces of paper that magical sentence:

Everything that happens to me is the best possible thing that can happen to me.

Place these pieces of paper where you spend time and will see them often—for example, on the bathroom mirror, in a prominent place in your car, where you work, on your wallet or purse, on your dresser, on the inside of your briefcase, in your locker or closet, on the refrigerator door, on the ceiling over your bed, on the wall in front of your desk, and in other places that are significant to you.

When you find yourself in a trying situation, that's when you go to work, reminding yourself of this truth and causing yourself to *act as though whatever is causing the difficulty is for your maximum benefit.*

Smile. Imagine the situation turning out wonderfully well for you. Act as though you have just been given some wonderful information or a genuinely appreciated gift. Switch any outgoing negative energy, which stems from your belief that what's happening is bad, to your most positive track. Affirm that what's happening is going to be of tremendous benefit to you. As a result of natural law, these new thoughts and actions will cause the continuing stream of events to unfold with the desired end—happiness.

The Universe doesn't make mistakes.

Everything is happening just as it should. It's only our perception of difficulties that causes us the distress and the difficulty we experience. Not only that, but when we label events as "bad," we fail to perceive the benefit that is waiting for us.

I once knew a man who lost his job, cursed his luck, and began to drink alcohol and snort cocaine. He went on a three-month binge. One day, toward the end of the three-month binge, he received a phone call from a company he had always wanted to work for. They had heard that he was available and wanted him to start right away. First, however, they asked him to take a drug test. They had high standards and didn't want anyone working for them who was using drugs.

He couldn't pass the drug test, so he never got that job. But the real reason he didn't get the job was that he had lost faith in the Universe, cursing his "misfortune" for having lost his job rather than expecting that the Universe had something better in store for him. In reality, when he lost his old job, it wasn't a mistake or a misfortune but a purposeful event. It was a graduation certificate that would allow him to move on to something better. He just didn't know it.

If you and I were living in a Universe that was not alive, conscious, and fully aware of us, it might be the case that "things just happen." However, we are an integral part of a Universe that is fully alive, fully conscious, and totally aware of us—a Universe that provides exactly what we need to achieve our full potential.

You are the Universe…a part of it.

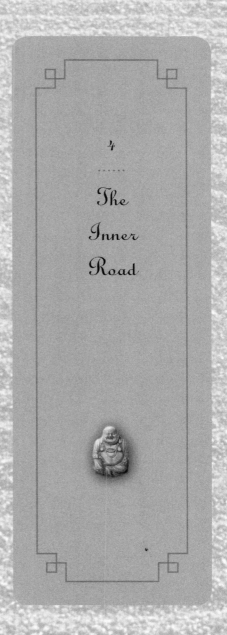

4

· · · · · ·

The

Inner

Road

*If you cannot find
the truth right where
you are, where else do
you expect to find it?*

—DOGEN

4 | the inner road

HAPPINESS COMES FROM WITHIN. IT IS A STATE that is produced by our minds. Although there are external objects and circumstances that can cause us to feel happy, the objects or circumstances themselves are not the cause of our happiness. The way we feel about those objects or circumstances—what our minds think about them—is the cause of our happiness.

Two simple examples will help to clarify that point. The first is an arena filled with thousands of people watching a sports event. When the game is over, some people are happy and some are unhappy, depending on whether the team each person favored won or lost. Being happy or unhappy about the result of a sports contest is an inner response to an outer event.

Neither happiness nor unhappiness is contained in the event itself.

Each spectator might hold some loyalty to a team or might have a financial interest in the outcome, pride in one of the players, or allegiance to the school or city the team represents. Those attitudes produce the response to the contest and to the outcome, not the event itself. If the essence of the event were happiness or unhappiness, everyone would feel the same way about the event. Thus, what determines each person's state of happiness or unhappiness is not the event itself, but what the event means to that person.

All the events of life work like that. It is the way you look at things and the way you relate to them that determines your state of happiness or unhappiness, not the things themselves.

Here's another example. Suppose there is a very large house being built next to the very small house in which we live. Let's say that we are unhappy because of the dust, the noise, and the prospect that this big house is going to be right next to ours, overshadowing it. Let's say that after a few months of experiencing discomfort, months that find us ever more unhappy about what is going on as our patience wears thin and the house looms larger, the contractor in charge comes to us and tells us that a rich relative of ours ordered the house built as a gift for us.

The same house, the same dust, and the same noise evoke a much different response from us after we receive this new information. We may still be annoyed by the conditions that exist while the house is being built, but the knowledge that the finished house will be ours far overshadows the temporary inconvenience.

The power of our mind to influence our thoughts and to make any two of us see the same thing differently is brought out in the famous Zen story about two monks looking at a flag.

One monk observed that the flag was moving. The other disagreed and said it was the wind that was moving. The sixth patriarch of Zen happened to be passing by and, hearing their argument, told them: "Not the wind, not the flag; mind is moving."

cause and effect

> *Your worst enemy cannot harm you*
> *As much as your own thoughts, unguarded.*
> *But once mastered,*
> *No one can help you as much.*
>
> —THE DHAMMAPADA

Since happiness and unhappiness are states of mind based on your interpretation of events (what you choose to see), you can change the state of your mind by supplying your mind with new information. You may not always have such direct information as being told that a new house is being built for you, but you can feed yourself new information by choosing new ways of looking at and interpreting the events of your life. When you do this, you will not only be able to survive even the most difficult of times, but you will also come through them with a smile on your face.

If you're not familiar with the term meta-physics, *meta* means "more than" or "beyond" and *physics* has to do with the physical world. So metaphysics is concerned with what's more than or beyond the physical world. Metaphysics is part of our effort as humans to reach beyond what we see, touch, taste, smell, and hear—to intuit what is beyond nature as we perceive it.

Through metaphysics, we discover the true nature of things, their ultimate essences and reasons for being. For me, metaphysics is a philosophy that incorporates the Universal laws that govern everything in the physical world. It also has to do with the unseen but perceived laws that regulate and control the world beyond the physical.

Here's a bit of metaphysical law that relates to one of the basic and most important aspects of our Universe—cause and effect. Simply stated, this metaphysical law says:

Every action produces a reaction, and that reaction is in exact accord with the action.

The metaphysical law of cause and effect applies

to your beliefs in the following way. Every belief that you hold manifests itself in some manner by either causing you to take some form of action or by preventing you from taking action. If you don't believe something is possible, you won't even attempt it.

In the early part of the twentieth century, there was a paradigm regarding the 4-minute mile. It was said, and almost everyone believed, that it was impossible for a human to run a mile in under 4 minutes. Doctors of that era said that the human physiology would break down and kill a runner before that could be accomplished. Engineers said that the aerodynamics of the human body made it impossible for someone to run a mile in under 4 minutes.

It seemed that this belief must be true because no matter how many thousands of runners attempted to break that record, they all failed. That's the power of a paradigm. It cripples everyone who believes in it and makes it seemingly impossible to break through to the other side. Yet on May 6, 1954, Roger Bannister ran a mile in 3 minutes, 59.4 seconds. He broke through the existing paradigm. Just six weeks later, John Landy, an Australian, ran the mile in 3 minutes, 58 seconds, and by the end of 1957, sixteen more runners had run the mile in less than 4 minutes.

Today, many runners regularly run the mile in less than 4 minutes, and one man, John Walker, has done so more than a hundred times. The current world record is 3 minutes, 43.13 seconds, held by the Moroccan Hicham El Guerrouj, who established it on July 7, 1999.

Once the old paradigm was smashed and a new paradigm was created, running the mile in less than 4 minutes became a common occurrence. It's not that the runners were faster or stronger; it's that they believed it could be done. That's what happens to a paradigm, and to any belief system, when a hole is blown in it. Everyone pours through the gap in the new way of thinking.

Now it is your turn to end any of your existing thought paradigms about what the events in your life mean, about how life "treats" you, or about the possibilities for happiness in your life. You can take charge of your own mind and impact how your life unfolds.

5
......

Mindful
Happiness

My mind is

the guiding-rein.

—THE BUDDHA

5 | mindful happiness

YOUR STATE OF MIND IS THE MOST IMPORTANT factor in the outcome of your life. When I talk about your mind, I'm not talking about your physical brain, that bundle of nerve tissue in the upper half of your skull, but rather about the part of you that thinks or observes. Even though you use the bundle of nerve tissue to think, there is a part of you—a separate part of you—that directs your thinking. That part of you may be outside your brain or inside it, or it may even be that you think with your whole body, which I'll talk about later in this chapter.

You've probably been aware of the part of yourself that's a "watcher," that seems to be standing back and looking on while you're engaged in your life. That is the part of you that contains your beliefs—what you believe to be true about the world in which you live, Universal laws, your fellow beings, your role in life, and your values. These beliefs make up what I refer to as "your personal philosophy."

Today there is much research showing the connection between our mind, our emotions, and our body. It is not a new concept. Gifted physicians throughout the ages have told their patients that one of the most important aspects of healing, if not the most important, is the will to live. Some 2,400 years ago, the Greek physician Hippocrates, who is considered to be the father of medicine, told his students that negative emotions cause disease and that positive emotions are a crucial factor in recovery.

If you are happy, energetic, and excited about an upcoming event, or generally in a hopeful state of mind, your body's immune system will be powerfully affected and will respond accordingly by keeping you in a state of optimum health. If you are despondent, sad, unhappy, lonely, in pain, or depressed, your immune system will respond powerfully to those emotions by mirroring your depressed state. In fact, modern research has shown that our thinking even influences the moment-by-moment reproduction of cells in our body. What follows is a simplified version of a complicated process, but bear with me, because this is an important link in understanding why what we think, feel, and believe are so powerful.

your body, brain, and beliefs

Think with the whole body.

— TAISEN DESHIMARU

There is a constant two-way communication going on between your body and your brain. Do you remember times when you've thought of something dire and had a "sinking feeling" in your stomach area? That's the kind of communication that goes on between brain and body.

Recent research has found that not only does your brain communicate with your cells, but your cells also communicate with your brain and other parts of your body. In fact, the latest discoveries by scientists are revealing that we think with more than just our brain; we think with our body as well. In fact, it is not inaccurate to look at our entire body as being part of our brain. That may be a new and startling thought, but don't reject it. Many scientists now believe that we're actually a "bodybrain."

A key part of our body's incredible communication system involves our cells' receptors. Every cell in your body can have millions of receptors on its face, and each cell has perhaps seventy different types of receptors. In the early 1970s, Candace Pert, Ph.D., was the first scientist to prove the existence of these receptors with her discovery of the opiate receptor.

The receptor molecules float on the cell's oily outer membrane and have roots that reach deep inside the cell. In her wonderful book *The Molecules of Emotion*, Dr. Pert says that "the life of a cell, what it is up to at any moment, is determined by which receptors are on its surface, and whether those receptors are occupied by ligands or not."[1] A ligand is a small molecule that binds itself to a cellular receptor.

There are three chemical types of ligands: neurotransmitters, steroids, and the ones we're most interested in right now, the peptides. According to Dr. Pert, as many as 95 percent of all ligands may be peptides. The receptors and their ligands, says Dr. Pert, "have come to be seen as 'information molecules'—the basic units of a language used by cells throughout the organism to communicate across systems such as the endocrine, neurological, gastrointestinal, and even the immune system."[2]

We now know that peptides are produced in the hypothalamus, an amazing gland in the center of the brain, and that the type of peptide produced is primarily determined by what we think and feel. The hypothalamus produces peptides that duplicate every emotion you experience, from anger, hate, sadness, frustration, and depression to joy, enthusiasm, and happiness.

The peptides are channeled to the pituitary

gland and then into the bloodstream, where they visit all twenty to thirty trillion cells in your body (about ten thousand average-sized human cells can fit on the head of a pin). The peptides dock onto the cells and create minute physiological phenomena that can translate "to large changes in behavior, physical activity, even mood," explains Dr. Pert.[3] The peptides, she says, "play a wide role in regulating practically all life processes."[4] When the peptides dock onto the receptors, they take control of all the cell's activities, including, among other things, commanding whether or not it will divide and the composition of new cells. It's like the captain of a ship stepping on board and beginning to give orders.

In the film *What the Bleep Do We Know!?*, Dr. Joseph Dispenza explains that when a new cell is produced, it isn't always a clone of the old cell but *a cell that contains more receptors for whatever peptide it received that caused it to split.* If the cell received peptides produced by emotions of depression, the new cell will have more receptors for depression and fewer receptors to receive feel-good peptides.

You rely on cell division for the reproduction, growth, repair, and replacement of damaged, worn-out, or dead cells. An estimated 300 million cell divisions occur every minute to replace cells that die. Each day, two percent of your blood cells die and are replaced by fresh ones. Every two months, you have an entirely new blood supply. Given what we now know about peptides, receptors, and the role of emotions and thoughts, you can see the chain of events that takes place *as new cells are created according to what you think and feel.*

If you feel depressed for an hour, you've produced approximately eighteen billion new cells that have more receptors calling out for depressed-type peptides and fewer calling out for feel-good peptides. It's as if trillions and trillions of receptors are all cupping their little hands around their mouths like tiny megaphones and shouting, "Send us more depression!" In short, thinking gloomy thoughts creates a body that is more able to feel gloominess than joyfulness. It also creates *the need* for more gloomy thoughts, and you become addicted to gloominess.

The total number of receptors in your body is beyond imagining. You are, in truth, one vast receptor. Taking the example of depression, you can actually become addicted to that state because your body is demanding more of what it's been receiving. It has literally developed an appetite for depression. If, on the other hand, your personal belief system causes you to be happy, your receptors are creating a body that is more able to feel happiness—and that wants to feel happiness.

The more you engage in any type of emotion or behavior, the greater your desire for it will become.

That is true for anything, from depression and addictions of all kinds to emotions like anger or happiness. We become addicted to anger, for instance, because of the psychological and physiological effect it has upon us. It produces adrenaline, a powerful stimulant. We actually become dependent on the emotion of anger for the stimulation it gives us, so we fight with our spouses, our friends, our fellow workers, and anyone else we can engage in a conflict.

It doesn't matter whether your craving is for emotions like excitement, anger, depression, or joy, or whether it is for the feelings you get from using addictive drugs or alcohol; the bottom line is that whatever you crave is a result of your bodybrain wanting and demanding it.

The impact of this information about how your thoughts and feelings create and condition your cells and how your cells communicate is staggering. Think about it. What did your cells' receptors communicate to the rest of your body all day today?

being susceptible to happiness

The highest nobility lies in taming your own mind. —ATISHA

The idea that you create yourself by what you think and feel is actually good news. Now that you know how your system functions, you can use your emotions and thoughts to create a body that's more receptive to feel-good states. There's only one way to do that—by feeling good. *The way to create a body that's more susceptible to happiness and less susceptible to sadness is to be happy.*

The importance of holding the right belief is also based on the fact that a part of your brain can't tell the difference between an imagined experience and an actual one. Some people who imagine hearing a piece of chalk making a screeching sound on a blackboard experience a shiver up their spine. For others, thinking of the taste of a lemon makes them pucker. Dreams are another good example. When the events in a dream frighten you, you feel just as frightened as if the events were happening to you in your waking state.

When researchers from Harvard University tested subjects using a brain scanner, they found that seeing a picture of a tree and imagining a tree activated the same parts of the brain.[5] In the same way, when you imagine that a condition you are experiencing can be cured, everything in you— your physical body, your immune system, your mind, everything—responds with healing energy, with a forward, impelling motion that says *yes* to a cure.

Your mind is powerful. You may have heard the saying "That which you can conceive, you can achieve." Or, as Henry Ford once said, "Whether you believe you can or you can't, you're right!" If you believe that a goal is possible, you will set out to accomplish it. If you believe that a goal is impossible, you will fail even to begin. In this state of mind, even if help is offered, you'll usually reject it because you still believe that the goal is unattainable.

Seven years ago, muggers wounded a man of about thirty. They slashed his arm with a knife and cut it to the bone from his shoulder to his elbow. Everything was severed—the veins, ligaments, arteries, muscles, tendons, and nerves. For several years after his wound healed, he continued to experience severe pains in his arm and shoulder. He sought help for the pain and his doctors prescribed Vicodin. It numbed the pain, but the pain returned when it wore off and therefore he continued using the drug.

As a consequence, he became addicted. Because he didn't want to remain hooked on Vicodin, he sought help from many neurosurgeons and psychiatrists. He visited fifteen neurosurgeons in a three-year period without obtaining relief. The last one told him, "Son, you have neuropathy. The nerves in your arm are degenerating and you'll have pain for the rest of your life. I suggest you go to a pain management clinic." The man was devastated by the news, but he refused to believe that he couldn't obtain relief.

About three years ago, he called Passages, the addiction cure center in Malibu, California, that I cofounded, and I took his call. I told him of our physical rehabilitation program and of our Director of Physical Rehabilitation, Dr. Lyn Hamaguchi, who was trained in the arts of acupuncture, acupressure, and healing by a doctor of traditional Chinese medicine from mainland China. I encouraged him to come to Passages and I told him of the wonderful cures that Dr. Lyn had helped to facilitate with acupuncture and acupressure. I told him that I would be surprised if she couldn't do the same for him, despite what he had been told by the neurosurgeons.

He believed me and enrolled in our program. In one treatment, Dr. Hamaguchi relieved him of most of his pain. He then found it easy to overcome his Vicodin addiction because he no longer needed it to relieve his pain. There was, of course, much more to his treatment than just acupuncture. He had to psychologically overcome the pain of the loss he felt at having taken three years to search for a cure, and he had to become reconciled to the memory of the attack and the anger he felt toward his assailants.

Can you imagine this man's fate if he had believed what the doctors had told him and had given up? He wouldn't have sought treatment, he might still be fighting his pain, and he might still be hooked on Vicodin or some other pain medication. Today he continues to be completely free of addiction.

worthy companions

Even if it is painful and lonely, associate with worthy companions. —DOGEN

Whatever you are trying to achieve in life, it is essential that you surround yourself with people who believe that what you seek and what you believe in are not only possible but also very probable. My son and I are the cofounders and codirectors of Passages Addiction Cure Center, which I spoke of earlier. The rate of success there is higher than at any other center or program we know of, and we have created a holistic three-step program that people can implement themselves by working with health professionals where they live. One of these steps works entirely with the power of the mind and beliefs. This step is essential to the success of those who attend our treatment center.

From the moment a client walks through the door, I and our team of therapists hold the intention clearly in our minds that he or she will return to a state of perfect balance, perfect health, and renewed zest for life. From our experience, the attitude of the client is extremely important, but so is the attitude of the healers and therapists. Practitioners who don't believe that a cure is possible will not talk about a cure, will not look for a cure, and will most likely fail to bring about a cure. Worse than that, they'll poison the minds of clients with the belief that a cure is impossible and that they are doomed to be addicts or alcoholics for the rest of their lives.

That belief results in a self-defeating attitude that undermines the great gains that are possible. The only time this poisoning would have a positive effect would be if someone got angry when told that rubbish, refused to accept that belief, and set out to prove the therapist wrong.

Would you really do your utmost to succeed in the treatment of any ailment if you believed that you were beyond all hope of recovery? What caliber of treatment would you expect from a therapist who believed that? How do you think your body and mind would respond if you were surrounded by psychologists, psychiatrists, or drug and alcohol counselors who subscribed to the belief that "once an alcoholic or addict, always an alcoholic or addict" and who believed that your current stay in rehab would be one of many?

You would immediately be deprived of hope. That is sad, because hope—the hope for a cure, the hope for a return to a normal, healthy life free from any challenging condition—is the most powerful stimulus for complete recovery.

Compare the misguided healers with healers and therapists who believe that a cure is possible. They will talk about a cure, will look for a cure, and will be more likely to bring about a cure. Most important, they will instill in their patients the belief that a cure is not only possible but probable and that their patients are definitely going to be among those who will be completely cured. That belief alone results in the self-empowering attitude that sets the stage for recovery. Each one of our team of therapists holds the vision of a complete cure for every one of our clients, and I believe that plays a key role in our high success rate.[6]

The previous example of curing an addiction can be applied to any and all areas of your life. If you are surrounded by people who not only don't believe in your goals and your positive outlook on life but who also continually try to tear you down, it will be extremely challenging for you to hold firmly in mind that you will succeed and that you can be happy.

Who you allow into the circle of your life will make the difference in the quality of your life. As the Buddha taught, "He who walks in the company of fools suffers a long way. Company with fools…is always painful; company with the wise is pleasure."

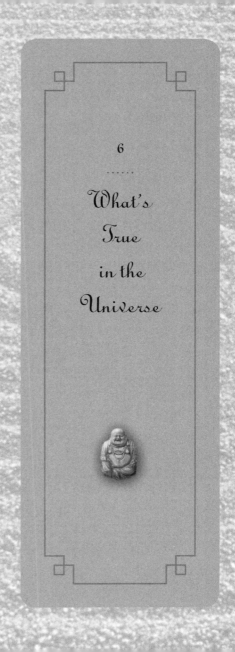

6

· · · · · ·

What's
True
in the
Universe

Obey the
nature of things,
and you will walk freely
and undisturbed.

— SENG-TS'AN

6 | what's true in the universe

THE ANCIENT SAGES LOOKED TO NATURE TO SHOW them how to live a life of happiness. They taught that oneness with nature and living in harmony with its ways are keys to inner peace. Understanding nature and the laws of the Universe can help you to understand your own essential nature, move with the cycles of your life, and reach the goal of happiness.

In this chapter, you will learn how to build a new personal philosophy for yourself based on what is true in the Universe. That's why it will work. Acting on the basis of that philosophy will create happiness. It works every single time—no exceptions.

The future may seem to you to be something unknowable, indeterminate, perhaps scary or hopeless, as if you're sitting in a buggy being pulled by a team of high-spirited horses without knowing how to control them. You don't know if those horses will turn your buggy over and spill you to the ground, drive off a cliff, become lost, or take you to your destination.

Not knowing how to handle them, direct them, or stop them, you can become terrified. But once you know how to rein in the horses and control them, they will follow your directions and take you where you want to go. You'll be relaxed and confident because you know you're in control of your journey. That's how life is when your personal philosophy is based on what is true in the Universe; you know what actions to take to bring about the circumstances you desire, and you are not disappointed.

Don't be concerned if you haven't been aware of these natural laws before. Once you begin to incorporate a philosophy into your life that is in accordance with Universal law, your life will bring you such joy that you'll laugh in amazement. It will be as if you've spent your life driving a car in reverse and you've suddenly discovered that there are gears that make it go forward—and fast!

To understand how the Universe works, it's necessary to come to an understanding of its essential nature. The Eastern sages who sought to live in harmony with the Universe realized that we are as integral to and inseparable from the Universe as are the stars, the mountains, the oceans, the great galaxies that wheel in space, and all else that exists. Just as our hands are part of us, we are part of the Universe—and just as we are aware of a touch on our hands, the Universe is aware of everything we experience, because we are part of it.

Everything is created from the same pool of energy, and except for the difference in the way everything appears, it is actually the same. You could compare it to water that is frozen into billions of different shapes; while the shapes appear to be different, they are all made from water.

Separation is an illusion.

The nineteenth-century Indian spiritual leader Swami Vivekananda put it this way in his book *Jnana-Yoga*: "There is but one Life, one World, one Existence. Everything is that One....Who can find any real difference between the wave and the sea?" Although the "whole universe is that one Existence," he says, "name and form have created all these various differences." Similarly, the Buddhist text the Bardo Thodol (more well-known as the Tibetan Book of the Dead) teaches that our minds create the illusion of separation and that our minds can free us from it as well: "Separation is untrue....The state of mind transcendent over all dualities brings Liberation. Again and again, look within thine own mind."

The Chinese philosopher Lao Tzu, who lived 2,500 years ago, also expressed that truth in his ancient classic the Tao Te Ching: "Existence is beyond the power of words to define....Whether a man dispassionately sees to the core of life or passionately sees the surface, the core and the surface are essentially the same, words making them seem different only to express appearance. If name be needed, wonder names them both: from wonder into wonder existence opens."[1]

your personal philosophy

Seeing through to essential nature is the window of enlightenment.

—HAKUUN YASUTANI ROSHI

Before we were born, our world, this planet Earth, existed. And there existed laws, Universal laws, that governed everything on, in, and around our planet, including us. Those laws were in place and fully operative before we were born, and they'll remain so during our lifetime and long afterwards.

Once we were born into that system, those laws made themselves known to us. If we thought we could walk through a tree and tried it, we quickly discovered we couldn't. If we thought we could fly like birds and we jumped from a high place, we quickly found we couldn't. If we thought we could make friends by bullying people, we quickly found that it didn't work, that we became disliked for our bullying tactics, or we saw that another person who used those tactics was disliked because of it. If we did something nice for someone, we saw that it was appreciated, and in that way we made friends.

Universal laws, unlike man-made laws, cannot be broken. That's fortunate for us because we can rely upon them and not be disappointed. One of these laws, as discussed earlier, is the law of cause and effect: *"Every action produces a reaction, and the reaction is always in exact accord with the action."* Throw a rock into a pond and it makes ripples—every time. The bigger the rock, the bigger the ripples. If you plant an acorn, you'll get an oak tree, not a willow. If you overeat, you'll get fat. If you're a mean person, you'll lack friends. If you fail to nourish yourself, you'll become ill. Ultimately, by the consequences you experience, the truth will make itself known to you.

If you're not now happy most of the time, it's because you are relying on something that you learned should make you happy but isn't, or there is a condition in your life that is causing you to feel unhappy. That condition could simply be the habit of being unhappy. It's true. Some of us have been unhappy for so long, with only rare moments of happiness, that unhappiness has become a habit, a natural condition. Based on the law of cause and effect, if you can discover the true cause of happiness, you can put that cause to work and, with absolute certainty, be happy. Just as importantly, if you can discover the cause of your unhappiness, you can learn ways to avoid bringing about that condition.

In short, if your personal philosophy is not in accord with Universal law, how could your efforts to be happy possibly succeed? To take a ridiculous example, if you believed that the way to rid yourself of a headache was to repeatedly smash your head with a hammer, you would soon discover that what you believed was not how the Universe works.

Because your belief was based on an assumption that was not in accord with Universal law, not only would your efforts fail, but you would also incur additional injury that would complicate the matter rather than resolving it. Just as you will fail to achieve a goal if you set out to accomplish it in the wrong way, so you will fail to achieve happiness if you go about it in the wrong way.

> *A personal philosophy that's based on what's true in the Universe will sustain you through every occurrence that life brings to you.*

It will save you from costly errors of judgment, countless hours of misery and needless suffering. It will help you see that events that you may have lamented for weeks, months, or even years are the best events that could have happened to you.

a curse or a blessing?

> *The sage blends everything into a harmonious whole. He is unmindful of the confusion and the gloom, and equalizes the humble and the honorable.* —CHUANG TZU

Each incident in life, even a painful experience, basically provides you with only two choices: you can either curse it and call it an "accident" or you can call it "good fortune." I've learned that there's only one of those two choices that can bring us happiness—and help us bring happiness to others. I've learned that bad events simply do not happen. This was brought home to me as never before when one day I found myself lying face down in the mud at the bottom of a deep ravine.

My son Pax and I were out gathering rocks for a landscape project. We were driving through a canyon in Malibu when I saw what looked like an interesting rock projecting eight or nine inches above the edge of a ravine. I got out of the truck and saw that the rock was about twenty inches long and embedded in the side of the ravine, which was about thirty-five feet deep. Holding onto the rock, I climbed into the ravine and kicked a place into its earthen wall to give myself a toehold so I could get under the rock and push it up. I was wearing tai chi shoes with smooth cotton soles, and the surface of the dirt was still moist from the morning dew.

The rock weighed well over a hundred pounds, but I managed to dislodge it. Then I heaved and pushed until I had it at its balance point, just ready to topple onto the road, when my feet slipped out from under me. I slid to the bottom of the ravine, still standing erect but supporting myself against the side of the ravine with my outstretched hands. What I didn't know was that the rock hadn't fallen onto the road but was hurtling down into the ravine, bounding into the air because of its triangular form.

The flat part of the rock hit me squarely on the top of my head. I was slammed into the ground with such force that two bones were broken in my left hand, and my knees were bruised from the terrific force with which I hit the ground. I was lying face down in the mud, unable to breathe and unable to move because all my vertebrae had been compressed and I was paralyzed.

Now, what do you think was going through my mind as I lay in the mud, paralyzed and unable to breathe? Before I tell you, I must go back in time so my answer will have some meaning for you and so you can begin to understand what I mean by a philosophy that is based on what's true in the Universe.

When I was in my teens and early twenties, I had no moral code whatsoever. My mother, Bea, was born in New York in 1900 to a poor German family. When she was fifteen, she was raped and became pregnant. They forced the older man to marry her and this began a life of hell. My mother hated him for what he had done to her, and he hated her because she immediately became as tough and as hard as was necessary to defend herself from him.

During the first two years of her marriage, she sewed buttons on shirts to earn a few pennies. After three years, she divorced him, but by then she had become totally hardened and she turned to a life of crime. Within a few years, she was leading a stolen car ring in New Jersey and had a crew of con artists working for her in New York City. When prohibition began, she became a bootlegger and supplied whiskey to the local clubs.

Later, when I was born, she brought me up the only way she knew—to be like her. She always insisted that I call her Bea, never mom or mother. The first rule she taught me, when I was about three-and-a-half, was "Never tell the truth." She said, "Only fools tell the truth. If you do, it will only get you into trouble." Her motto was "Never tell the truth when a good lie will suffice." So I lied and cheated and stole, and I was highly praised for it.

She taught me shoplifting when I was four. It was one of her favorite games. She also told me that no one could be trusted, particularly women, and she taught me not to respect authority. Regarding rules, she explained that the main rule was that there were no rules except the "golden rule," which was "Those who have the gold make the rules." When I grew older, my business dealings were always shady.

Fortunately, I was an insatiable reader, and in the many hundreds of books I read, I perceived a different way of life. When I reached the age of twenty-five, I began to realize from the books I had read that Bea, that marvelous woman whom I loved dearly, had programmed me one hundred and eighty degrees in the wrong direction. I was following a path that would unerringly lead to unhappiness for me and for everyone around me. At first, it was hard to see that, because she was so successful and had become something of a minor political power. Besides that, Bea was fun-loving and generous to a fault. I, too, was successful, although I had obtained my success in deceitful ways.

So I set out to change my ways. I realized

that I couldn't do that living near Bea, so in 1965 I packed up and moved to California. I was determined to turn my life around. My first resolve was that I would always speak the truth. My second resolve was that I would never again take advantage of anyone. This wasn't easy for me in the beginning since I had lived my whole life up to that point lying and without a moral code, and I had to make one up as I went along.

As the years passed, I made some progress. If I lied to someone, I would force myself to go to that person and tell him or her the truth. I made a trip back to New Jersey to make whatever amends I could to the people I had wronged and cheated. That part was very difficult, but I forced myself to carry on until I had seen everyone I could remember having hurt in some way.

from perfect to perfect

One in all,
All in one—
If only this is realized,
No more worry about your not being perfect!

—SENG TS'AN

When I was about thirty-three, I came across an ancient Chinese book of wisdom called the I Ching. When writing came to China five thousand years ago in 3000 B.C., the I Ching was the first thing to be written. Before that, it had been passed along in the oral tradition for thousands of years. The I Ching may be the world's oldest known wisdom. It survived all those years because it was of such great value to the people. I studied it not only because of its wisdom, but also because it contained many Universal laws. As the I Ching was written so long ago, much of its language and meanings were unclear to me, and I yearned to know what its phrases meant. I felt certain that some of the secrets of the Universe were locked away in them.

Over the years, I grew in my understanding of Universal laws such as cause and effect, and I became ever more careful of my words and actions. I learned that character is the bow from which we shoot the arrows of the future. During all those years, I spent several hours each day studying the I Ching, and I still spend a few minutes each day reading it.

I came to see that Universal law governs

everything. Once I understood that, I was able to perceive and understand a great many other aspects of the world in which we live. For instance, I learned that *all the laws of the Universe are in favor of the continuation of the Universe.*

How do we know that to be true? Because the Universe continues. Astronomers and scientists tell us that the Universe has been around in its current state for about eighteen billion years. If there was even one law that favored discontinuation, surely that would have come to pass by now. Since it hasn't, I feel it is safe to believe that all the laws are in favor of continuation.

For the Universe to continue to exist, it can only permit the best possible events, perfect events, to occur at any moment in time. If it were otherwise, the Universe would be in danger of its own destruction because one imperfect event could lead to two imperfect events, to three, and so on unto destruction. Imperfect events are not tolerated, not even once. Since our Universe has continued for all those billions of years, there can be little doubt about the perfection of its construction. The Universe continues to be perfect at every moment and never permits even the first imperfect event to occur. It goes from perfect to perfect to perfect.

This is related to the Universal law of the conservation of energy: *"Nothing can be lost or destroyed, only changed."* That includes us. Being part of the Universe, we will continue to exist. Perhaps we will exist in a different form, perhaps in a different state, but exist we shall.

When the time comes for us to leave our physical bodies, we may keep our personalities and our souls, so to speak, or we may not. Perhaps we will simply merge into the totality of the Universe. Yet it's actually not accurate to say that we will merge with the totality of the Universe because we are never unmerged from it. And who's to say we shall not come back to this planet again? Perhaps we will reemerge once again on earth. We may have forgotten how we came to planet Earth, but we certainly know the way to get here, evidenced by the fact that we are here.

In any case, we'll continue in some form or another—every end being glorious. The greatest honor one can have is to be part of the Universe. To additionally have been chosen to receive the degree of awareness we have is a wondrous gift, wondrous almost beyond belief.

Carrying further the thought that the Universe is constructed so that it will continue to exist, it can be said that the Universe wants to benefit itself to the maximum amount possible at all times. Since we are an integral, inseparable part of the Universe, the same thing applies to us.

Everything that happens to us is for our complete benefit.

Even if an incident hurt us or took something from us, that event will always work to our benefit since the Universe will not let anything bad happen to itself, and we are part of "itself."

By studying these Universal laws, I came to see the entire Universe as alive and aware, a living, breathing entity that has consciousness—that *is* consciousness. That is why I capitalize the word *Universe*. What most people refer to as God, Allah, Jehovah, Buddha, or any of a thousand other names used to refer to a supreme entity, I simply think of and refer to as "the Universe," a vast energy source of consciousness. As the decades have moved on, I have continued to live with my philosophy and it has borne itself out through every circumstance of my life, even when what I believe has been put to the fire, sometimes on a daily basis.

what good thing will come of this?

The only way to make sense out of change is to plunge with it, move with it, and join the dance.

—ALAN WATTS

Now that you know my state of mind when I found myself plunged to the bottom of the ravine as the rock smashed me to the ground that day, I ask you again: What do you think was going through my mind as I lay in the mud, paralyzed and unable to breathe? I suppose I've given you too many clues for you not to have some inkling of what was going through my mind. What I was thinking was "I wonder what good thing will come from this?"

Pax had seen the rock disappear over the side of the hill. He ran to the ravine, looked down, and saw me lying in the mud. He slid down, turned me over, and asked if I was okay. I was able to speak because my paralysis was only from the neck down, and I told him I didn't know.

As I lay there, I began to get a tingling sensation all over my body, the kind you feel when your foot has gone to sleep or you hit your funny bone. My vertebrae began to decompress and I was slowly able to move. I didn't want to reach up and examine my head because I was afraid I would put my hand through the hole I thought must have been there and kill myself. When that rock had landed on my head, it sounded as if someone had broken a baseball bat over my head. I didn't think anyone could get hit that hard and survive.

One week later, I was lying in bed recovering and I opened up a copy of the I Ching to read. Suddenly, the passages that had earlier baffled me were now understandable. Somehow, that blow to my head had opened the channels that allowed me to perceive the meanings of what had before been unintelligible. Since that time, I've written ten books on the I Ching, including my own popular version of it called *The I Ching: The Book of Answers*, written under my Chinese pen name, Wu Wei. All that was a result of the rock smashing my head.

We can speculate forever about whether that rock falling on my head was divine intervention or an accident without any significance, but the benefit to me was beyond calculation. My main study up to that point in my life had been to try and fathom the information locked away in that ancient Chinese volume, and suddenly I could understand it! For that kind of gift, I would willingly be hit on the head many times.

Because the core of my personal philosophy is that everything that happens to us benefits us, I was also spared the futility of cursing my bad luck, lamenting the occurrence, or feeling as if I was a victim. The reason I was able to benefit from my accident was because of the way I looked at the event. Not for one instant, then or now, did I think anything other than that this so-called accident was for my total and complete benefit.

If I hadn't viewed this event in a positive light, I would have been looking for all the bad outcomes, and in so doing I could have actually created problems for myself. My stress over what had happened could have led to sickness and further complications with my neck. I could have been depressed and cursed my bad luck. Yet none of those things happened. Oddly enough, to this day I have no neck pain, nor have I lost mobility of any kind, and I even get to put the incident to good use by writing about it these many years later.

7

......

Adapting
to
Change

Flow with

whatever may happen

and let your mind be free:

Stay centered by accepting

whatever you are doing.

This is the ultimate.

— CHUANG TZU

7 | adapting to change

A PHILOSOPHY OF INCESSANT CHANGE WAS AN essential part of the ancients' understanding of the Universe. Change, explains the I Ching (literally "the Book of Changes"), is a constant—we can count on that. All of nature is in a state of growth and flux. Thus, another piece of wisdom about happiness that comes from the tradition of the I Ching is this:

A situation only becomes favorable when one adapts to it.

Here's an example of how adapting to changing events and looking at them in a positive light can create a positive outcome. Twenty-four years ago, I bought a brand-new car and it was parked in the alley next to my house. I walked out of the house just in time to see an old VW bus scrape the front fender of the car. The driver got out, threw his hat on the ground, then hung his head, holding it in his hands. He obviously had no money to pay for the damage to my car and he almost began to cry. His wife was in his car and his son was in the back seat crying. When the man saw me coming, he looked even more distraught. I walked up to the car, looked at this man, and said, "Perfect. That's just what my car needed."

He couldn't believe what he was hearing. I told him to have a nice day and not to worry about the scrape, that now I wouldn't be so worried about getting a scratch on my car. He began crying tears of happiness and hugged me.

He danced a little jig and ran around to his wife and hugged her. He got his family out of the car and introduced me to them. He told me that he had just arrived in town, that he was a carpenter, and that they were looking for a place to stay until he could find work. I gave him the phone number of a friend of mine who was in the construction business, and the next day he began working for my friend.

Three weeks later, this man showed up at my house to give me two hundred dollars to repair the scratch. I told him to keep it. I said that I liked the scratch because it reminded me of what a wonderful place the Universe is. To me, it was worth the damage to my car just to see how happy that man was when I told him that his scratching my car was a perfect event. I still think about it to this day and it still makes me happy.

I never did repair the damage. When people would ask me how I scratched the car, I would say, "It's a gift from the Universe." When I was asked to explain what I meant by that, I would tell them of my philosophy, and I was able to lead many people into a new way of understanding that stood them in good stead. On several occasions, the people I had spoken to told me that they had come to see seemingly bad events in their lives as a "scratch on the fender."

Suppose I had not reacted the way I had when my car was scratched. Suppose I had instead punched the driver of the VW bus and after a violent fight we had both wound up in jail. Suppose I had been sexually molested in jail, had gotten into another fight, had seriously hurt someone, and had been sentenced to twenty years in prison.

Again, all of life presents us with two basic ways to treat events. We can either label them "good for us" or "bad for us." The event is only an event. It's how we treat the event that determines what it becomes in our lives. The event doesn't make that determination—we do.

a change in outlook

He who has once known the contentment
that comes simply through being content
will never again be otherwise than contented.

—TAO TE CHING

In the Far East, there is a line of thinking that equates happiness with knowing what you can do without. To put that Far Eastern thought another way, happiness is being happy with what you have. The Tao Te Ching explains: "Embrace simplicity.... Be content with what you have and are, and not one can despoil you."

Most Westerners do not subscribe to that way of thinking. We want more of what we want and less of what we don't want. To us, having and not having are the major causes of our happiness or unhappiness. Not having enough of the basic necessities such as food, clothing, or shelter can cause unhappiness. Poor health can be a cause of unhappiness. Unfulfilled desires—such as unrequited love, not being able to take a vacation, not having a good car, not having other possessions we desire, not having enough money to pay bills, not being able to do the things we want, or not having the time to do them—are major causes of unhappiness.

Having those desired things may make you happy, but there is no certainty that they will. Many people who have those things are quite unhappy. If you think of people you have known, you are likely to recall some who got the very things they wanted but found no lasting happiness as a result. So where is the true source of happiness? The answer is probably clear by now:

> *The true source of happiness is within each of us.*

Happiness comes from our response to the conditions of our lives. We are powers in and of the Universe. We are able to think, to do, and to create. It is only past conditioning that has taught us to be unhappy about unfolding events. If you respond by being happy, you *are* happy.

In the mid-eighties, I led workshops for people who wanted to change their lives. Those workshops showed me once again how happiness comes from within us and how important it is to have a strong personal philosophy that can sustain us through whatever life brings our way.

The workshops were incredibly successful in that the participants made lifestyle changes and accomplished deeds they had previously believed were far beyond their capabilities. They made advancements in their chosen field of work, they moved out of apartments and bought houses, they overcame lifelong fears, they ended dependent relationships with family members and friends, they accomplished long-sought goals, they became happy and free of bad habits, they discovered their passion for life, and they found peace.

Watching their successes, I saw how essential it is to live according to an empowering personal philosophy, a lodestar, a guiding light that will see us through the difficult times of despair, hardship, grief, and despondency that seem to regularly occur to us all. It became clear that those who led fulfilling lives had adopted a philosophy that changed their down feelings into cheerful feelings and brought a smile to their faces, a smile that was more than just a brave veneer in the face of adversity.

I understood that a strong philosophy based on what is true in the Universe is so powerful and joy-giving that it withstands all the rigors and tests of time. Further, I came to realize that a weak philosophy is a weak way of life. I saw that the failures that had dogged the footsteps of my workshop participants had always been due to a weak or misguided philosophy. Once they adopted the new philosophy and put it into action, their lives took an amazing turn for the better. As their outlook changed, all the circumstances of their lives changed.

Just as it was true for those workshop participants, it is true for you:

How you conduct yourself along the path that is your life determines how your life unfolds.

That's another basic law of the Universe. You, and you alone, determine what your world is like. You are the doorway through which your life unfolds.

Imagine if you were angry most of the time. Your anger would affect everything and everyone around you. People wouldn't want to be near you. The anger would also produce an acid reaction in your body that would slowly destroy you. It would influence your thinking so that you wouldn't have the state of calmness necessary to produce clear, rational thinking. You would have few friends, if any. You wouldn't enjoy eating or recreational activities. Harmony would be absent from your life. You wouldn't be able to feel happy, and it would probably be difficult to get a good night's sleep. In business, success would be hard to come by or it might not come at all. If you worked for others, it would be hard to keep a job. As the Samurai maxim goes, "The angry man will defeat himself in battle as well as in life."

freedom from the tyranny of events

> *To find perfect composure in the midst of change is to find nirvana.* —SHUNRYU SUZUKI

A strong personal philosophy does more than sustain us through the tragedies of life. It also sustains us daily in everything we think and do. It gives us optimism and hope. It frees us from the tyranny of events. Here's a story from those workshops I offered that shows how liberating it is to be free of the events that knock on our door. (It's a little like the story I told earlier about my car but with a slightly different twist that shows how this philosophy can help lift you up in so many ways.)

Doris was a waitress in a coffee shop. She came to the workshop because her son had been there the month before and the results he had experienced amazed her. One day, after she had been in the workshop for about three weeks, I arrived and saw fifteen or twenty of the workshop participants in the parking lot looking at a new car. They were laughing and talking excitedly. When they came in, I asked what the excitement was about and they all laughed.

Doris had bought a new car the day before, and when she had gone down to the garage in her condominium complex that morning, her new car had a dented fender. Doris said that ordinarily she would have cried, gone back upstairs, gotten back in bed, pulled the covers over her head, and stayed there all day so that no more bad luck could come her way.

However, she remembered what she had learned in the workshop, and she looked at the car with new eyes. That dented fender no longer had the power to ruin her day. She reported that she had just experienced one of the best days of her life because she was no longer tied to what she called "the tyranny of events," those incidents that come to all of us—the lost watch, the stolen wallet, the missed bus or plane. Doris said she might not even get the fender fixed because it had such great meaning for her. She was free, and everyone outside who was looking at her dented fender and seeing her reaction to it was rejoicing in her freedom and in their own.

dealing with trauma

When you can be calm in the midst of activity, this is the true state of nature....When you can be happy in the midst of hardship, then you see the true potential of the mind.

—HUACHU DAOREN

Each of us has suffered in our lifetime. We've been lied to, we've been betrayed and cheated, and we've been taken advantage of. Many of us, perhaps you, have been beaten, raped, mistreated, forced to do things against our will, or sexually molested by parents, siblings, or strangers. We've had our hearts broken and we've suffered great financial, spiritual, and physical losses. We've grieved over the loss of loved ones and we've been born with physical or mental deformities. How we deal with those traumas and conditions and others like them will determine our state of happiness today or, for that matter, any day.

A few years ago, Peter, a twenty-five-year-old athlete, checked into Passages Addiction Cure Center. He had been using marijuana. Peter was particularly interested in my weekly metaphysics sessions. He loved the philosophy portion of those groups and took it to heart. He and I also had several one-on-one sessions. In those sessions, he learned what you're learning here. At the end of his thirty-day stay, his marijuana addiction was over. A few months after he left the Passages treatment center, Peter had an accident and is now paralyzed from the waist down and confined to a wheelchair.

Two days after his accident, I went to see him in the hospital. When I walked into the room, his eyes lit up and he said in a quiet voice, "I know this is the best thing that could have happened to me." Today, Peter persists in that belief. We talk every few months and he tells me of the heights to which his enlightenment has soared. He says that his spiritual growth could never have come so far in such a short time without his accident.

He's an inspiration to all who meet him and

he occasionally visits us and speaks at meetings of Passages alumni. He has come not only to understand but to live in harmony with the Universal law that a situation only becomes favorable when we adapt to it. "If you laugh at misfortune, you will not be overcome by it," said the great Tamil poet-sage Valluvar. "Misfortune may rise like a flood; but bold thoughts will quell it. If you refuse to be grieved by grief, then grief itself will grieve."

How did you feel about Peter's response when I walked into his hospital room and he said, "This is the best thing that could have happened to me"? Did you say to yourself, sarcastically, "Yeah, right!" as if nothing could possibly be further from the truth? To the degree that you reacted that way, your personal philosophy is different from the one that's sustaining Peter and his peaceful feeling while he sits in his wheelchair. It means that you probably regard all incidents that seem unlucky as actually being unlucky. But it's mainly because of that kind of thinking that circumstances in your life have come about.

A strong philosophy based on what's true in the Universe will save you from playing the role of the victim—a person who's been ill-used, a person who's suffered bad luck, or a person whose life is one of despondency and unhappiness. A strong philosophy will sustain you through adversity because you know that the mystery will unravel itself and reveal a happy and perfect ending.

Do you think that you could maintain Peter's joyous outlook if you became paralyzed? If you don't have a personal philosophy that will see you through the times of hardship, tragedy, and despair that come to us all, it's unlikely.

the worst of times, the best of times

> Know all things to be like this:
> A mirage, a cloud castle....
> Nothing is as it appears.
> —THE BUDDHA

I've learned firsthand how good things can emerge from even the hardest of times if we maintain a strong personal philosophy. I watched this process unfold with my son Pax. Pax began using marijuana, along with an occasional beer, when he was fifteen. I did what I could to deter him from that behavior, but he continued. At the time, I didn't know that that seemingly harmless behavior could escalate into hard drug use. When Pax was eighteen, he came home from school one day and began crying. He told me he was hooked on heroin.

For the next six years, I battled heroin for Pax's life. I put him in thirty-day programs, sixty-day programs, and ninety-day programs. Nothing worked. He was clean forty times or more. Each time that he relapsed, I would ask, "Why?" Each time, he did not know the reason, except to say it was the incredible high. It was as if he was powerless to resist the temptation. I was constantly afraid I would lose him, and I never knew from one day to the next if I was going to see him again.

I took him to drug therapists, alcohol therapists, psychologists, psychiatrists, addiction specialists, and counselors of every sort. They all had suggestions for rehab, twelve-step programs, and more counseling, but not one of them was really seeking to discover *why* Pax was using heroin. In nearly every case, their suggestions were directed to creating an environment where he would be less apt to use heroin, and they advised me to punish him for his bad behavior. I learned, however, that punishment doesn't work as a means to correct substance abuse, even when someone is facing death.

Case in point: during Pax's years of addiction, a gang of drug dealers drove him into the desert to kill him because he had stolen drugs from them. They forced him to dig his own grave. Somehow, he talked them out of killing him by convincing them that he could get the money. The day after that harrowing experience, he was using heroin again. When Pax's jaws had been broken in two places from being kicked in the face by a drug dealer who wanted money from him, he had to go to the hospital to get his jaw wired shut. His teeth were pointing in all directions, he was barely able to speak, and he had to sift food through his teeth. He came home from the hospital in that wretched state and I hurried over to see him. I walked in the door and, unbelievably, through his wired jaw, he was smoking heroin again.

At one point, determined to break the cycle of heroin use, I took him away with me to an isolated cabin in the Big Sur mountains on the coast of California. I kept him absolutely clean for nine months. The first week we left Big Sur, he used heroin and cocaine.

I believed that Pax was turning to heroin for a reason. I did not know what the reason was, but I believed there was one. In his drug-free days before he became dependent, he was athletic, outgoing, happy, and a good student, even achieving a student-of-the-month award. He wanted to stop using heroin and cocaine and return to a normal life, but he was unable to stop. Yet I never gave up hope. I never stopped encouraging him to keep searching for the real, underlying cause of why he was turning to addictive drugs. One day, at last, Pax discovered the "why" behind his dependency. That was the last day he ever used drugs or alcohol. In that moment, he was able to free himself of his addiction.

Today, Pax is whole in every way—healthy, happy, prosperous, clear-minded, completely cured, and helping others to achieve the same freedom that he has achieved. It was Pax's idea to open the Passages treatment center. When he had finally let go of his dependency, he said to me,

"Look, we know how to do it—let's do it."

So together, my son and I founded and are now codirectors of Passages, where we work side by side every day. I see him, and I'm proud of him and of what he has accomplished and is accomplishing. He has been reclaimed from the land of the dying, from an addiction to alcohol and addictive drugs that was so powerful that at times it seemed impossible to save him. Yet save him we did. All credit to him and to the generous and loving Universe of which we are all a part.

During our journey to hell and back, Pax and I learned many things about the world of alcoholism and addiction. We researched everything we could find about treatment programs, alcoholism, and addiction, and we learned by experience what did and did not create lasting recovery, both in Pax's life and in the lives of others in treatment. When nothing else worked, we created a holistic, hand-tailored program that saved Pax's life. At Passages, he and I use what we learned in curing him to help others discover the roots of their addiction or alcoholism and break free.

To some, Pax's years of addiction and trauma may seem like an irretrievable loss. Yet if you were to ask Pax how he sees the ten years of his addiction—the beatings, the degradation, the humiliation, the loss of friends, the loss of his college years, the loss of respect, the lost years—he would tell you that it was the most terrible experience of his life and the greatest. He would tell you that those ten years led him to his life's work, that without them he would never have had the idea or the drive to create Passages, and that the Universe was preparing him for a brilliant future where he could save the lives of thousands. He would go on to say, and I've heard him say it, that if he had to go through it all again to achieve what he has now achieved, he would do it. It was the worst of times; it led to the best of times.

Not only that, but as a result of this experience, I was able to write the book *The Alcoholism and Addiction Cure: A Holistic Approach to Total Recovery* to help others achieve a cure. In it, Pax tells his story in detail and I share the keys to recovery we discovered. The book shows people how they can use the same guidelines we use at Passages—the same keys that helped Pax recover—to put together their own personalized, holistic treatment program with the support of health professionals where they live. Out of our struggle and trials, we can now give hope and life to others.

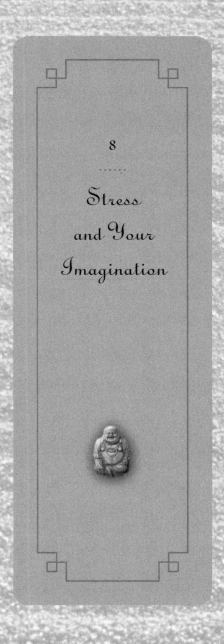

8

. . . . . .

Stress

and Your

Imagination

Those with limited views

are fearful and irresolute:

the faster they hurry,

the slower they go.

—SENG-TS'AN

8 | stress and your imagination

ONE OF THE GREATEST OBSTACLES BETWEEN YOU and happiness is stress. By stress I mean a feeling in your mind of fear, anxiety, distress, worry, unease, or foreboding caused by using your mind to imagine a bad outcome to a past, present, or future event or situation. Nothing else causes stress. The events or the situations do not contain stress, although they seem to.

Stress comes from the way you relate to events or situations.

Sound familiar? It should, because it's the same formula as the one for happiness. Neither stress nor happiness is contained in things, events, or situations. Things are just things, events are merely events, situations are only situations. It's up to you to supply your reaction to them. You get to choose.

To prove to yourself that this can be the case, think of the many times you have felt stress over something that never materialized or, if it did materialize, ultimately turned out to be for your benefit. If only you had known from the beginning that it would work out favorably, how much more pleasant your life would have been. That's the way you can approach all situations.

Stress will never be completely gone from our lives because of all the negative programming we have taken on, but we can eliminate most of it. The tricky part in eliminating stress is controlling our imaginations to envision a happy outcome rather than a poor one.

How do you come to believe that the stressful situation will ultimately turn out to be to your advantage? The short answer, and the one I explored in greater detail in chapter 6, is that because we *are* the Universe, a part of it, and because the Universe wants to benefit itself to the maximum amount possible at all times, the positive outcome is the only outcome it will permit.

I realize that may still be a big leap for you to take, especially considering what's gone before in your life, but that's the leap you need to take if you are to be stress-free and happy most of the time. Only when you put that belief into practice are you able to perceive it as reality. After you have practiced for a while and have seen the results, you'll come to know it's true. And that's when you'll begin to wear that little smile—often.

expectations

You should not be surprised at whatever you see or hear....If you are ready to accept things as they are, you will receive them as old friends.

—SHUNRYU SUZUKI

You create your world by your expectations, and you can influence the future by how you respond to the present. To help eliminate stress from your life, now or in the future, rely on your philosophy. If, as part of your philosophy, you believe that every event will turn out for your benefit, stress will never enter the picture. I have spent weeks convincing people in my workshops of that truth, and when they finally came to believe it, stress was largely gone from their lives. Many of those whose lives had been nearly ruined by stress said it was the greatest gift they had ever received.

If you stay in control of your imagination, it's impossible to feel fear or stress. You should get a great deal of comfort from that information because your imagination is entirely under your control. You can just as easily imagine a good outcome as a bad one. Here's an example so you can see what I mean.

Let's say that you and I are living in a house that's in foreclosure. We haven't made our mortgage payments for six months, the bank has foreclosed on us, and the sale is set for next month. After the sale, we'll have to move out, and we have no place to go. Over the past months, we've fretted and anguished, moaned and lamented. Every bit of the discomfort we're now feeling has been caused by our imagining a bad outcome.

Now, suppose that unbeknownst to us, Aunt Agatha passed away a year ago and left us a fully paid-for house in the country along with enough cash to keep us living quite comfortably for the rest of our lives. When we find out about Aunt Agatha's bequest, we suddenly use our imagination to create a wonderful future for ourselves—a life of ease in the country. We couldn't care less about the impending foreclosure. We go out and celebrate for several days.

Then Aunt Agatha's lawyer calls and tells us that there's been a mistake. Aunt Agatha didn't leave the house and money to us; she left it to our sister. Now we're back to where we were in the first place, imagining a very bad outcome. On top of that, we have the loss of Aunt Agatha's house and money to lament.

For a week, we imagine all the bad things that will happen when we're thrown out onto the street with no place to go. Then the lawyer calls again. Our sister, who hated Aunt Agatha, wants no part of the house. She wants us to have it, along with all the cash. Now we're back to joyously imagining a good outcome. We move out of our foreclosed house and into the country house—only to find that it's uninhabitable and in a bad neighborhood.

The lawyer calls again. There's been a glitch in the will and the cash is going to be held up indefinitely. We go into a slump and start imagining the terrible time that lies ahead. The next day, we get an offer from a developer who wants to develop the entire area. He offers us a huge sum of money for the house. We're elated, imagining that our troubles are finally over. . . .

Well, you get the picture. What has caused us our grief and our joy? We have! By using our imaginations. We've been bobbing along like corks on the ocean, rising and falling as events have gone up and down. Just for a moment, imagine what it would have felt like and been like in our imagined story *if we had known from the first moment* that everything would turn out wonderfully well for us. That's the way it will feel when your philosophy is based on what's true in the Universe and when you expect that whatever you are going through will turn out to your advantage, even if you don't yet see how that is possible.

You may remember things that have happened to you that seemed bad at first and that still appear to be bad. That is probably because you have continued to treat what happened as "bad" and thus your actions have brought about that result. It's not too late to make a shift. Change the way you are thinking about what happened and the results will change as well.

obstacles

Chilling autumn rains
Curtain Mount Fuji, then make it
More beautiful to see.

— BASHO

Another part of a strong and healthy philosophy that allows us to create happiness in our lives has to do with how we look at obstacles. One of the reasons any obstacle is in your life is so that you can grow from it and become strong. You know the old saying that a chain is only as strong as its weakest link. Well, you're only as strong as your area of greatest weakness.

You can see those principles at work in nature all the time. A mother bird pushes her young out of the nest so that they will learn to fly. She stops feeding them so that they will have to venture forth. Baby lions playfully attack each other, even if the one being attacked doesn't want to play, so that they'll learn how to fight for a mate when they come of age. In the animal world, the survival of the fittest is the law. The stragglers and weak animals are driven off or killed. Only the strongest males get to mate with the females.

Life in the animal kingdom is hard, and that's what makes animals so strong and so capable. In fact, everyone and everything that is alive today is only alive because its ancestors were survivors. Thus, one of the reasons that the circumstances of your life are sometimes so painful, so devastating, and so difficult is this:

The Universe always strikes at your weakest point because that's what most needs strengthening.

Your challenges are, in effect, hand delivered by a loving Universe to make you stronger. In order to get the benefit from the obstacles, face and overcome them rather than turning away from them and giving up.

Here's an example. One of the most common causes of anxiety is speaking in front of groups of people or meeting other people we don't know. This anxiety comes from using our imagination to foresee a bad result. For instance, some people, including actors, become addicted to tranquilizers, which they say they need in order to perform, speak in front of groups, or even attend big meetings.

They do not *need* a tranquilizer, even if that's what a doctor told them. What they need is to work on strengthening the inner weakness that is causing them to imagine a bad outcome. Perhaps they simply need to overcome their fear by practicing public speaking in order to become better at it and more confident. Yet instead of dealing with the real reasons for the anxiety, they are turning to a drug to take the anxiety away. By using drugs, they are depriving themselves of the opportunity to grow into strong public speakers.

How should you deal with the challenges in your life? First, recognize that the situation or event has a purpose and that it is meant to benefit you. The circumstances may look like problems, feel like problems, and seem to be problems, but that's just one possible point of view. Once you learn to look at your problems as "workout situations," they take on a whole new aspect. I call them "workout situations" because they are just that: situations you can "work out" with so that you can gain strength and understanding. After you have done that, the circumstance is of no further use to you and it passes out of your life.

Of course, the relief and the answers won't be handed to you without effort on your part since it is by working your way through the problems that you will gain strength, wisdom, and knowledge. Realize also that the goals you seek aren't the be-all and end-all of life, even though you may think they are.

It's the path itself that's the be-all and end-all. Reaching for your goals and searching for answers is what is leading you along the path you've chosen for this lifetime. The path itself is where the truth is to be found, where your destiny manifests itself, and where your happiness lies.

progress

The miracle is not to fly in the air or to walk on the water, but to walk on the earth.

— CHINESE PROVERB

Earth is a place of discovery and of experience. It's no accident that you're here. It's no accident that you're reading this. You're a spiritual creature, here on earth to perfect yourself. Your problems and what you've suffered were and are in your life for that purpose. If you leave the planet without discovering that vital piece of information, your life will have been like driving two thousand miles to see the Grand Canyon and then spending your entire vacation in a hotel room. If you believe that your existence is just life and death and that everything in between is only a struggle, your life will lack the magic that makes life vital, wondrous, and transcendent.

Having said that, you can never really be off your path to enlightenment—your path to realizing that you are an integral and vital part of the Universe. Enlightenment is like an ocean, and our paths to enlightenment are like rivers.

Each river is different, but they all eventually lead to the ocean. No matter what we're doing or when, or whether it brings us happiness or remorse, gain or loss, we're all on our individual paths to enlightenment. Even when we've done something we consider wrong, we're still on our path to enlightenment.

The progress you make on your path will either be quick or slow, according to your awareness. If you're lying drunk in the gutter, chances are that your progress will be slow. If you're intentionally seeking enlightenment, which manifests as a desire to discover your relationship with the Universe, you'll use your so-called problems as opportunities to learn and you'll progress quickly. As a result, you'll enjoy the rewards of peace, success, abundance, great good fortune, and well-being.

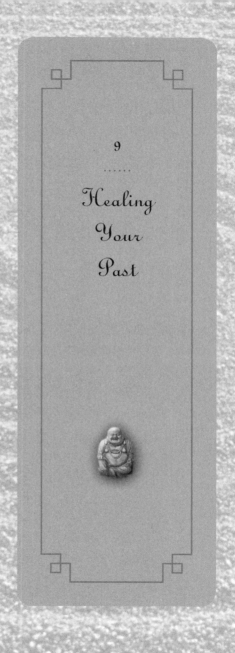

9

......

Healing

Your

Past

Do not pursue the past.

Do not lose yourself in the future.

The past no longer is. The future

has not yet come. Looking deeply at life

as it is in the very here and now,

the practitioner dwells in

stability and freedom.

— BHADDEKARATTA SUTTA

9 | healing your past

WE HAVE NOT LEARNED HOW TO ROLL TIME backward to undo or change events of the past. However, we can change the way we feel about past events so that they stop tormenting us in the present—so that they stop spoiling "now."

We all carry around a lot of hurtful baggage from the past: slights, intentional transgressions against us, broken hearts, hurt feelings, memories of people who cheated us or lied to us or betrayed us, events that brought us pain, missed opportunities, seemingly wrong choices we made, lost objects, things we did or didn't do, misunderstandings that caused us pain or the loss of friends, things we did that brought hurt, pain, or disappointment to others for which we feel regret—the list is nearly endless. Carrying that load of hurtful baggage from the past is a useless burden we would be much better off without.

Healing the past enables you to be happy in the present.

How can you heal the past? You can shine the light of your new understanding on past events that have hurt you. You can open to the idea that whatever happened to you in the past eventually turned out or will turn out to be a benefit to you.

It is essential for your abundant happiness that you use your memory to go back into your past to the time when you were a child. Then, slowly coming forward, remember all those key experiences and relive them—except that at the conclusion of each event, you must make it right in your heart and mind.

That means you forgive yourself for the things you regret having done to others, you forgive others for the things they did to you, you acknowledge the rightness of the events that you thought did not benefit you, and, more than that, you acknowledge that each event was for your benefit or will turn out to be for your benefit—even if it was to strengthen a weakness or teach you a needed lesson, one that you can now share with those who are hopeless and hurting. Shining the light of your new understanding on those events is the magic wand that can change the hurt or regret you feel into feelings of acceptance, peace, and happiness.

Intentionally supplying your memory with new information causes you to feel differently about the past events of your life, which causes you to feel happy when you reflect on the past rather than to feel hurt. Once you have done that, each time one of those events comes to mind, use your new philosophy to remind yourself that the event was for your total and complete benefit. Remind yourself not to feel bad about it but to acknowledge the event as being the best possible thing that could have occurred to you and to everyone else at that time. That is hard to do, and it takes tremendous perseverance, but once you have tried it, you will see that the effects are colossal.

You can be happy if you are willing to let go of your past and leave yourself unencumbered so you can fly freely. It is so good to leave all that "stuff" behind. It's like walking away from a mountain of problems that will never again bother you. Can you see yourself doing that? Walking away from a mountain of problems that will never again bother you? When the weight of all that excess baggage has been thrown overboard, you can soar, light as a feather in a soft breeze, happy in your eternal now.

the present moment

The present moment is a wonderful moment.

—THICH NHAT HANH

The sages emphasize that another key to healing our pasts and living a happy life is living in the "now." The I Ching teaches: "The superior person sees and understands the transitory (that which passes) in the light of eternity."

We imagine an endless future stretching out ahead of us and an endless past stretching out behind. We believe that where we exist is the moment we call now, a moment that is a tiny hairline separating the future from the past. In actuality, the reverse is true; all there is and was and ever will be is an endless now. Is it not always now? The wise ones understand this truth:

This moment we call now is all that exists.

When we live in the now, keeping our awareness and concentration on the present moment, as Zen encourages us to do, we rein in our runaway imaginations—not dwelling on the past, not worrying about the future, not judging events as they come and go. As quoted earlier, Alan Watts, the renowned twentieth-century interpreter of Asian philosophies, said that "Zen is simply...that state of centeredness which is here and now."[1]

Zen's emphasis on meditation is aimed at that very point; meditation is a technique to keep us in our center, concentrating on the present moment. This practice gets us in the habit of viewing life itself in the same centered and balanced way—observing rather than reacting, resisting the impulse to judge events as bad. Buddhist leader Thich Nhat Hanh says that "meditation is not an escape from life...but preparation for really being in life."

Alan Watts likened the practice of living from our center to martial arts, where we are encouraged to "stay always in the center position, and stay always *here*." He says, "If you expect something to come in a certain way, you position yourself to get ready for it. If it comes another way, by the time you reposition your energy, it is too late. So stay in the center, and you will be ready to move in any direction." When living from your center, in the now, he adds, "you stand a much better chance of being able to deal with the unforeseen than if you keep worrying about it." [2]

Meditation does not have to be long or complicated for you to receive its benefits. If you haven't done it before, I suggest you begin by meditating for five minutes a day. A good time to engage in this practice is in the morning just after you've awakened, but you can do it at any time that works for you. Find a comfortable position where you are sitting with your spine straight. Close your eyes and concentrate on your breath.

Just follow your breath in and out for five minutes. If you find that you have started to think of something other than your breath during those five minutes, gently pull yourself back to concentrating on your breath. What you are seeking is five minutes of relaxed, easy focus on your breath. In, out, in, out, in, out. Summarizing how important this centeredness practice is, the Zen master Pao-chih simply said, "If the mind is never aroused toward objects, then wherever you walk is the site of enlightenment."

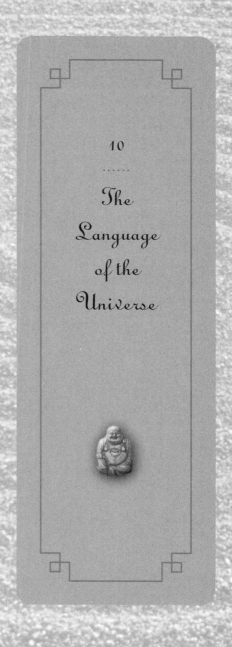

10
......

The
Language
of the
Universe

To those who

have conformed

themselves to the Way,

the Way readily

lends its power.

—TAO TE CHING

10 | the language of the universe

LEARNING TO BELIEVE THAT THE UNIVERSE IS alive, conscious, and aware and, more particularly, aware of each of us, can change your experience of life. It can change your relationship with the Universe in a way that will find you living in a brand-new world—one that will delight you as long as you are on the planet.

Not only is the Universe aware of us, but it also communicates with us. We, in turn, are constantly in communication with the Universe through our words, thoughts, and actions. The Universe responds with events.

Events are the language of the Universe.

The most obvious of those events are what we call coincidence. We're thinking of someone, the phone rings, and it's that person. We're trying to locate someone whose address we've lost and we meet a friend who says, "Guess who I saw yesterday?" Even as you are asking who your friend saw, your friend speaks the name of the person you are trying to find and is soon supplying you with that person's address and telephone number.

A couple I know were living in a remote part of Hawaii. The road leading to their house was one that only four-wheel drive vehicles should drive on, and it took two hours to get from the main road to the house. They desperately needed a four-wheel drive van. They talked to each other about how badly they needed that dream van, but there was only one of that type on the island, and it was not for sale. Even if it had been, they didn't have the money to buy it. Their only asset was a piece of land in a remote part of Montana, worth about ten thousand dollars. After their conversation, the wife silently added that it would be nice if her dream van was white and had a great stereo system.

Two weeks later, a white van of the exact type they needed approached their house. The driver said she was lost. She told them that she had taken the van to the island intending to stay, had changed her mind, and was leaving. The wife said, "That's good, because you're driving my van." As payment, the woman took the land the couple owned in Montana and paid them some cash besides. As it turned out, the van had a special stereo system.

Coincidence?

No. Communication from the Universe. It was a Universal event and *it happens to all of us all the time*. Communication from the Universe is continuous, although some communications are more obvious than others. Most of the time, we're not aware of these communications, or we may just think of them as luck or a quirk of fate.

In so doing, we miss what is truly the chance of a lifetime. Just by acknowledging the Universe when we become aware of such an incident, the Universe *increases the obvious communications*. What a treasure!

The importance of establishing that type of communication with the Universe cannot be overstated. That piece of information, along with the knowledge that the Universe is alive and aware, ranks at the top of the list of the small amount of information I've accumulated in my lifetime. It's like walking along with a two-year-old with whom you believe serious conversation is impossible. If it were possible, you could give the child important information that would be of great assistance, but you don't because of the child's supposed inability to understand what you say. Suddenly, the child looks up and asks if you believe that animals can think. A whole new world opens, and you begin to have a conversation with the child that is rewarding to you both.

It's just like that with the Universe: once the Universe becomes aware that you are aware of it and of its language (events), the communications increase, both in quality and quantity. You receive enormous help and input, and even the smallest bit of assistance from the Universe is of great significance in your life.

How can you acknowledge these communications? Just a simple knowing smile is enough, a nod of the head, an inward saying of "thanks," or, if you're more demonstrative, a whoop and a holler. Once you have put acknowledgement into practice, the results are powerfully gratifying and you become increasingly aware of the intimate relationship you share with the Universe. That's a comfort, a joy, and a great blessing.

the secret and the smile

Never say, "I cannot"; for you are infinite. Even time and space are as nothing compared with your nature. You can do anything and everything.

— SWAMI VIVEKANANDA

That single statement in chapter 1 of this book— "Be happy"—means choosing to be happy whenever you have the choice. It is not a mindless happiness, but a mindful happiness because it is based upon the knowledge that whatever happens to you will benefit you—and benefit you greatly.

Most of the time, we respond to life without taking a moment to choose the way we want to think and feel about a particular event or situation. It takes work to make the choice. A deliberate mental effort is needed to pause, reflect on the situation, remember the goal to be happy, consider the other choices, then choose to feel happy about whatever the situation is, knowing it will ultimately be to our benefit.

The hardest work comes when the situation is hurtful or has taken something from us or there seems to be some impending mishap in store for us. At that moment, choosing to be happy may seem impossible, but many people have learned to do it and they will tell you that the result is worth any effort necessary.

You can do it.

Those who have chosen to be happy walk about wearing a tiny smile that seems to indicate that they have a secret, the contemplation of which is making them happy. The smile may be in the mind only, but it is there. No matter what happens, the knowledge of that secret keeps the little smile in place. It's as though you were out walking and lost a hundred dollar bill, but you knew you had a few million dollars in the bank. The loss of the hundred dollars is inconsequential in the face of the knowledge that you still have several million left. The loss doesn't dim your happiness. In fact, the realization that the loss has not dimmed your happiness is by itself enough to make you happy—to know that you are past being bothered by things like that.

Once that secret is in place, you will find yourself enjoying the little things of life: you'll stop to admire a sparrow, a sunset, a breeze moving the leaves of a tree, someone's pretty hair. You'll enjoy a shower more than you did before, a walk, a conversation with a friend, or simply sitting, thinking about how wonderful the Universe is. You'll stop focusing on things that are detrimental to your happiness, on unpleasant events in distant places that can't possibly have an effect upon you, on dark items in the news, on inconsequential things that used to trouble you but now, in the knowledge of your secret, no longer take your attention.

The nagging worries that all is not right, that something bad is going to happen, that you might fail, that you might not be good enough, strong enough, bright enough, or own enough will disappear. The doubts will be replaced with the confidence that

You, as part of the Universe, are cared for as if you were a precious jewel, which you are.

Of course, you are here to learn. Of course, there are lessons. Of course, there are hurts and heartaches. Of course, the inevitable mishaps will occur. But you will see them with new eyes. That stubbed toe or lost wallet or lost job will no longer be a case for anger or pain because you know that you are being attended to by a benevolent and caring Universe. You will see through the disguise of misfortune to the heart of the truth, which is that these events have occurred only so you could be benefited—and benefited greatly. That is when the real happiness comes, the kick-up-your-heels, laughing, joyful kind of happiness that does not dissipate with time but grows ever more satisfying.

That's the way it is once you have come to realize the great Universal truth: everything that happens to me only happens so that I can be benefited to the maximum amount possible.

the great promise of the universe

See for yourself. —SHOITSU

What you have now, after reading this little book, is intellectual knowledge. It will not be of much value to you until you put it to use. Remember that the way of Zen means doing anything and everything with a particular concentration and awareness of mind.

Concentrate your mind, focus your attention on the great promise of the Universe, and say to yourself:

"Everything that happens to me only happens so that I can be benefited to the maximum amount possible."

Or say the short version:

"This is for my benefit."

Allow yourself to wonder, with expectancy and excitement, *"What good will come from this?"*

Treat unfolding events on the basis of the promise of the Universe and you will find yourself living in a world that is marvelously, miraculously better than you have ever imagined it, and you will achieve the goal of abundant happiness.

Don't start with what's most difficult—infant death, the tragic loss of a loved one, Hitler, or 9/11. Start with something small. When you have stubbed a toe, say, "Thank you for my stubbed toe. Right there is an acupuncture point that needed release. Now I'll have more energy!" If you bump your head, say, "Ouch, I bumped my head! I must remember to pay attention and stay present in the moment. Thanks for the reminder." Practice on little things, and what seemed impossible will soon be just as easy.

Thank you for spending this time with me. I acknowledge you for your marvelous effort. I respect you for persevering on your path toward enlightenment. I bow low to you for your greatness of spirit, your warrior's heart, and your search for the truth of your existence. May you attain to greatness, may your life be long and happy, and may you mount to the skies of happiness as though on the wings of six dragons!

Chris

notes

CHAPTER 5 | *Mindful Happiness*

1. Candace B. Pert, *The Molecules of Emotion: The Science Behind Mind-Body Medicine* (New York: Touchstone, 1997), 24.

2. *Ibid.*, 27.

3. *Ibid.*, 24.

4. *Ibid.*, 25.

5. G. Ganis, W. L. Thompson, and S. M. Kosslyn, "Brain Areas Underlying Visual Mental Imagery and Visual Perception: An fMRI Study," *Cognitive Brain Research* 20, no. 2 (2004): 226–41.

6. For more on the Passages Addiction Cure Center's program and approach, see Chris Prentiss, *The Alcoholism and Addiction Cure:*

A Holistic Approach to Total Recovery (Los Angeles: Power Press, 2007). Also see the following websites online: www.TheAddictionCure.com and www.PassagesMalibu.com.

CHAPTER 6 | *What's True in the Universe*

1. From *The Way of Life According to Lao Tzu,* translated by Witter Bynner, chapter 1.

CHAPTER 9 | *Healing Our Pasts*

1. Alan Watts, *What Is Zen?,* in *Eastern Wisdom* (New York: MJF Books, 2000), 55.

2. *Ibid.,* 53, 52.

acknowledgments

I am deeply grateful for the exceptional efforts of Nigel J. Yorwerth and Patricia Spadaro of PublishingCoaches.com as they helped shape this work and shepherd this book through all of its stages. I am indebted to Patricia for her expert organization of the material and for her enlightened editing and enhancements that captured the spirit of this work. I thank Nigel for putting together a great publishing team and for his unwavering efforts in promoting my work, helping me to get excellent distribution, and presenting my work to foreign publishers.

I also wish to acknowledge Roger Gefvert for his stunning and meticulous interior design, Nita Ybarra for her artful cover, and Martha Lonner and Kathy Lange at Media Works for their patience and skill in layout and production.

other titles from power press

Available from your favorite neighborhood and online bookstores

The Laws of Love: Creating the Relationship of Your Dreams,
by Chris Prentiss
Trade Paperback, $12.95

The Alcoholism and Addiction Cure: A Holistic Approach to Total Recovery
Breakthrough 3-Step Program from the World-Renowned Passages
Addiction Cure Center, *by Pax and Chris Prentiss*
Trade Paperback, $15.95; Hardback, $24.95;
10-CD Audio Version read by the author, $39.95

Be Who You Want, Have What You Want: Change Your Thinking, Change Your Life, *by Chris Prentiss*
Trade Paperback, $15.95

Meditation on the Perfect You
Companion CD to *Be Who You Want, Have What You Want,*
by Chris Prentiss
1 CD, $9.95

The Little Book of Secrets: Gentle Wisdom for Joyful Living,
by Chris Prentiss
Trade Paperback, $9.95

The I Ching: The Book of Answers, NEW REVISED EDITION
The Profound and Timeless Classic of Universal Wisdom, *by Wu Wei*
Trade Paperback, $18.95

A Tale of the I Ching: How the Book of Changes Began
An Enchanted Journey into the Origins and Inner Workings of the
I Ching, *by Wu Wei*
Trade Paperback, $10.95

**I Ching Wisdom, Volume One: Guidance from the Book of Answers,
NEW REVISED EDITION**
Practical Insights for Creating a Life of Success and Good Fortune,
by Wu Wei
Trade Paperback, $12.95

I Ching Wisdom, Volume Two: More Guidance from the Book of Answers, NEW REVISED EDITION

Universal Keys for Creating Peace, Prosperity, Love and Happiness, *by Wu Wei*

Trade Paperback, $12.95

I Ching Readings: Interpreting the Answers, NEW REVISED EDITION

Getting Clear Direction from the Ancient Book of Wisdom, *by Wu Wei*

Trade Paperback, $14.95

I Ching Life: Becoming Your Authentic Self, NEW REVISED EDITION

by Wu Wei

Trade Paperback, $12.95

The I Ching Workbook, NEW REVISED EDITION

The entire text of *The I Ching: The Book of Answers* and over 100 workbook pages to record your answers, *by Wu Wei*

Trade Paperback, $19.95

The I Ching Gift Set

The newly revised and updated edition of *The I Ching: The Book of Answers* + 7" yarrow stalks, *by Wu Wei*

Trade Paperback, $39.95

The I Ching Workbook Deluxe Gift Set

The entire text of *The I Ching: The Book of Answers* and over 100 workbook pages to record your answers + 10" yarrow stalks, sandalwood incense, Auroshikha incense holder, and silk I Ching cloth, *by Wu Wei*

Trade Paperback, $49.95

50 Yarrow Stalks from China

Handpicked by farmers in northeast China specifically for use with the I Ching

(50) 7" yarrow stalks, $19.95

(50) 10" yarrow stalks, $22.95

Bookstores, please contact SCB Distributors toll free at 800-729-6423.
Tel: 310-532-9400. Fax: 310-532-7001. Email: info@scbdistributors.com
Website: www.scbdistributors.com

For foreign and translation rights, contact Nigel J. Yorwerth
Email: Nigel@PublishingCoaches.com

about the author

Chris Prentiss is the cofounder and codirector of the Passages Addiction Cure Center in Malibu, California, and the author of *The Alcoholism and Addiction Cure: A Holistic Approach to Total Recovery*. He has also written a dozen books on Chinese philosophy and personal growth. He is known worldwide for his interpretations of the I Ching that make this ancient and sometimes difficult-to-understand subject easy to use and apply. Prentiss has led personal empowerment workshops in southern California and has written, produced, and directed a feature film. He resides with his wife, Lyn, in Malibu, California.